it's great fun!

Contents

Horribilly's Music
By Michaela Morgan

Cooking with Horribilly

Jellyfish Stew
By Jack Prelutsky

Soapy Steve
By Jess Mikhail

T0385948

See you inside

Horribilly's Music

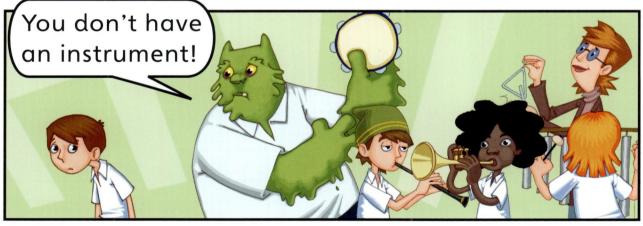

6

Cooking with Horribilly

It's fun to make a cake!

Weigh things - don't just tip them in the bowl!

1

Crack the eggs NEAR the bowl. Look out for bits of shell!

2

3

Mix it all up with a spoon ...

4

... not your hands!

Jellyfish Stew

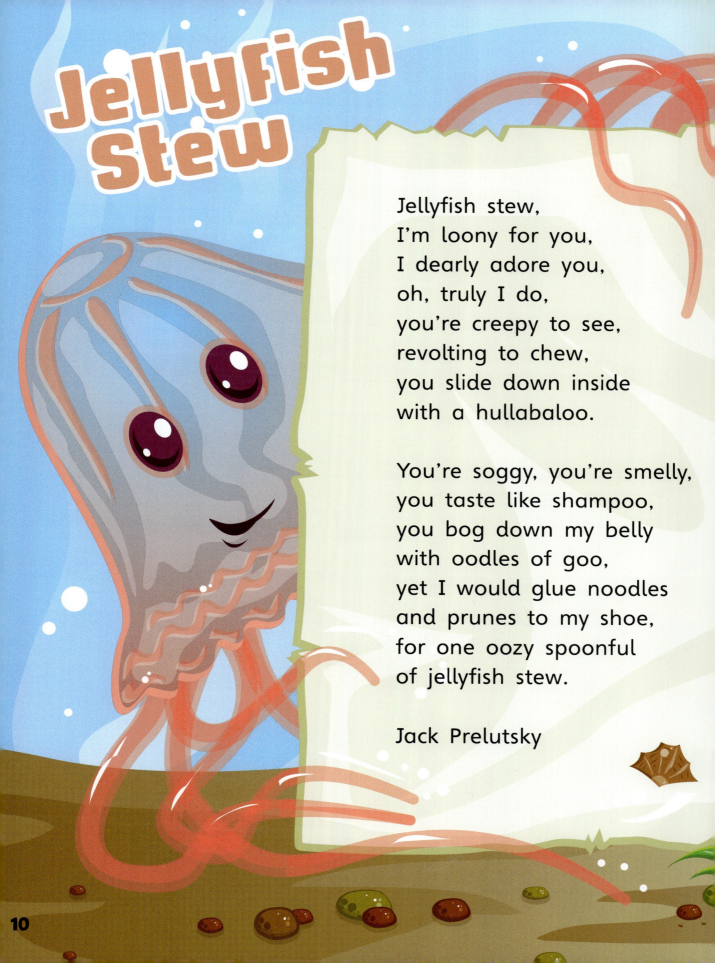

Jellyfish stew,
I'm loony for you,
I dearly adore you,
oh, truly I do,
you're creepy to see,
revolting to chew,
you slide down inside
with a hullabaloo.

You're soggy, you're smelly,
you taste like shampoo,
you bog down my belly
with oodles of goo,
yet I would glue noodles
and prunes to my shoe,
for one oozy spoonful
of jellyfish stew.

Jack Prelutsky

Soapy Steve

Steve – a boy who turns into a Soapy Hero!

Before

After!

Steve plays hide and seek ...

Where can I hide? Hmm ...

Later ...

Steve! Where are you?

SOAP POWDER

Steve?!?

SOAP POWDER

Next day ...

What's up, Steve?

It's a long story ...

Ben and Steve get on the bus.

Suddenly ...

SPLAT

What's happening?

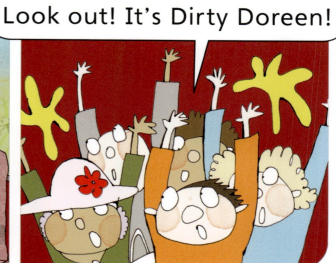

Look out! It's Dirty Doreen!